Facing Forward in Older Adult Ministry

Resources for the Congregation

OLDER ADULT ISSUES SERIES

The Office of Older Adult Ministry of the Presbyterian Church (U.S.A.) and Geneva Press are grateful for the generous gifts of many individuals, congregations, and organizations that helped make possible the publication of this series.

Facing Forward in Older Adult Ministry

Resources for the Congregation

S. Miriam Dunson

Published for the Office of Older Adult Ministry,
A Ministry of the General Assembly Council,
Presbyterian Church (U.S.A.)

Geneva Press
Louisville, Kentucky

ISBN 0-664-50089-7

Contents

Introduction

An Older Adult Affirmation of Faith

We believe that God is doing a "new thing," that it is no mere accident that at this time in history God is calling mature people, even those of advanced years, to participate in a living, growing, wondrous, creative activity that will breathe new life into the church and the world.

We believe that each of us has been given potential and possibility, that Christ has shown us the way to invest these gifts in God's Kingdom.

We believe that it is the task of the faithful people of God of all ages to sift through the dirt of life, to dig deep and uncover the talents with which we have been gifted.

We believe that through the power of the Holy Spirit, it is our joy and praise to offer back to God the best of what we have been given.

—Donna Coffman, Richmond, Va.

God is indeed doing a "new thing" in the church, in the nation, and in the world. That "new thing" is the unprecedented increase in the number of older persons who are living longer, healthier lives and who are eager to "breathe new life into the church and the world."

In 1776, only 2 percent of the population in the United States was age sixty-five or older. By 1890, it had increased only to 4 percent. The 1990 Census counted 31.1 million persons sixty-five or older, or 12.5 percent of the population. The projection by the Census Bureau is that by 2030, when all baby boomers will have reached their sixty-fifth birthday, 25–30 percent of the population will be sixty-five or older. An example of this rapid growth is reflected in the fact that during the 1980s alone, the older population increased by 22 percent. This will increase even more rapidly between 2010 and 2030, when the baby boomers turn sixty-five. During those years, the older population will grow by 76 percent while the population under sixty-five will increase only 6.5 percent.

The fastest growing age group in the nation is that of persons age eighty-five or older, the number having doubled between 1980 and 1990. However, this increase is not a phenomenon limited to the United States, but rather a worldwide phenomenon.

The United Nations recognized the significance of this phenomenon and passed a resolution naming 1999 as the International Year of Older Persons under the theme, "Toward a Society for All Ages." In that resolution, it is stated that over the next few decades, the number of people in the world over sixty will triple, causing the global percentage of older persons to jump from 9 percent in 1990 to 16 percent in 2030. The result will be a global society that is by far the oldest in the history of the world.

In the Presbyterian Church (U.S.A.), the Presbyterian Panel reports that 67 percent of all Presbyterians are forty-five or older, and that 35 percent are sixty-five or older.

The median age in the Presbyterian Church is fifty-four, although the median age in the nation is thirty-nine.

Because of these indisputable facts, it cannot be "business as usual" in the churches, in the nation, or in the world. We live in a society and nation, and serve a church, that idolizes youth and youthfulness, that sees aging as something to be denied, ignored, and covered up. We are inundated daily through all channels of advertising with age-defying miracle drugs and cosmetics designed to hide the signs of aging. Therefore, the first step that must be taken in combating ageism, and in seeking a new way to view our own aging process, is education.

The General Assembly of the Presbyterian Church (U.S.A.) designated 1998–99 as the Year with Education, and one area in which a massive educational process is needed is that of aging for all ages, and ministry with, by, and for older adults. It is with this thought in mind that this book has been developed, an annotated bibliography of books, videos, papers, and other materials to use as resources to enhance your library, and educate yourself, your family, and your congregation about what this new phenomenon means—to be an aging congregation in an aging society.

Two actions taken by the Presbyterian Church (U.S.A.) in recent years emphasize the fact that ministry with, by, and for older adults is crucial to the future of the church.

1. In 1992 the General Assembly of the Presbyterian Church (U.S.A.) adopted the Report of the Task Force on Older Adult Ministry, setting forth seven priority issues

with encouragement to focus on those issues for the next decade. Those issues are:

—Education and Leader Development
—Special Focus on Issues of Racial Ethnic Persons
—Attention to Health Care and Housing
—Education and Action Concerning Abuse of
  Older Adults
—Emphasis on Intergenerational Experiences
—Attention to Spirituality and Aging
—Global and Ecumenical Concerns

2. In 1998 the General Assembly of the Presbyterian Church (U.S.A.) adopted a resolution in response to the United Nations resolution naming 1999 as the International Year of Older Persons, commending the United Nations for its action and encouraging the church to pursue appropriate ways for its recognition and celebration. The resolution encourages congregations to engage in programs that bring different generations together for interaction and appreciation of one another. It also encourages presbyteries and synods to support older adult ministry in congregations, provide opportunities for older adult ministry leadership development, and provide resources. Theological seminaries are encouraged to include courses in older adult ministry in their curricula and to provide opportunities for exposure to older adult ministries through field education experiences and internships.

The resolution further states that during this International Year of Older Persons, special attention will be given to the situation of older persons, to preparing the population for the later stages of life, and to making this preparation an integral part of social policies. This preparation must encompass physical, psychological, cultural, religious, spiritual, economic, and health factors.

During this special year, Presbyterians and others in the community of faith can model the values that grow out of our biblical and theological faith traditions:

> —to lead the way in developing a growing respect for the dignity of all persons, regardless of age.
> —to lead the way in helping persons to live the entire span of life abundantly and to the fullest extent of their capabilities.
> —to shape values and attitudes in society, and to address issues concerning the meaning of life and the meaning of death.
> —to utilize the vast treasure of skills, wisdom, commitment, time, and energy found among older adults in leading the church into the next century.

In order to address this monumental need for education and action concerning the issues of older persons, and for ministry with, by, and for older adults in congregations, many resources are needed. In an effort to provide what are seen to be the best resources available, we offer this collection of annotated resources arranged around the seven priority issues.

1 Education and Leader Development

"They will still bear fruit in old age,
they will stay fresh and green."
Psalm 92:14 (NIV)

This priority issue is designed to provide leader development and continuing education of the church as a whole and especially of persons interested in and/or engaged in ministry with older adults, including older adults themselves. The purpose is to raise awareness of the needs and skills of older adults and to promote a better understanding of the role of the church and its leaders in meeting the growing needs of the very diverse older adult population. These books may be helpful in accomplishing these purposes:

Atchley, Robert C. *The Social Forces in Later Life: An Introduction to Social Gerontology.* 3d ed. Belmont, Calif.: Wadsworth Publishing Co., 1980. (Order from Wadsworth Publishing Co. 10 Davis Dr., Belmont, CA 94002.)

This is a basic text for serious students on issues of

The first seven headings listed are the seven priority issues approved by the 1992 General Assembly for the focus of the Presbyterian Church (U.S.A.) in older adult ministry for the next decade. The other items are arranged according to general topics.

aging. The text deals with how the economy, the government, politics, and community attitudes affect the lives of older persons. At the same time, Atchley looks at the scope of social gerontology, how to go about its study, and his future expectations of the field of gerontology.

Cole, Thomas R. *The Journey of Life: A Cultural History of Aging in America.* Cambridge and New York: Cambridge University Press, 1992.

This very interesting book gives a cultural history on aging and also enters into a dialogue about the meaning of life in the later years. The author includes a study on attitudes toward aging and older persons throughout history.

Dychtwald, Ken. *Age Wave.* Bantam Books, 1990.

This book is guaranteed to hold your attention as it presents the changing demographics of older adults in American society. The author projects future trends that will influence our lives, and writes specifically about the myths of aging, the new leisure, reworking work, reinventing the family, and even redesigning America. A must for anyone interested in older adult ministry.

Fischer, David Hackett. *Growing Old in America.* London and New York: Oxford University Press, 1978.

Although this book was published in 1978, it remains vital today. Written by a well-known and respected historian, this would be helpful reading for anyone involved in working with older persons, or looking at his/her own aging process. The author traces the changes and patterns of aging and views of the aging process from early America (1607) to the twentieth century.

Fowler, Margaret, and Priscilla McCutcheon, eds. *Songs of Experience: An Anthology of Literature on Growing Old.* New York: Ballantine Books, 1991.

This is a delightful compilation of writings by well-known personalities about the later years of their lives. Writers include Helen Hayes, Eleanor Roosevelt, Alice Walker, and others.

Hooyman, Nancy R., and H. Asuman Kiyak. *Social Gerontology: A Multidisciplinary Perspective.* 2d ed. Boston: Allyn & Bacon, 1991.

This social gerontology text presents the diversities of both the aging experience and the older population in a multidisciplinary manner. It includes an examination of the social lives of older people including a look at the historical, cultural, biological, physiological, psychological, and social contexts of aging, focusing on the significance of interaction between older people and their environments.

Seymour, Robert E. *Aging without Apology.* Valley Forge, Pa.: Judson Press, 1995.

Encouraging a positive approach to living as an older adult, the author discusses self-image, spiritual growth, coping with change and retirement, maintaining good health, integrating past and present, and contemplating death by celebrating life. The author challenges many of the common assumptions and misconceptions about aging.

Hayflick, Leonard. *How and Why We Age*. New York: Ballantine Books, 1994.

Written by an outstanding gerontologist, this book defines the difference between biological and chronological age, and then looks at how our understanding of aging has changed through the years. This book will dispel many of the most persistent myths of aging. It is well organized, comprehensive, and very informative.

Kimble, Melvin. *Aging, Spirituality and Religion*. Minneapolis: Fortress Press, 1995.

This book examines the ways religion and spirituality are experienced by aging persons within an aging society. Well-known contributors from a variety of disciplines explore this new terrain of an emerging interdisciplinary field. This book will function as a standard reference work and an important tool for professionals and students in health care, psychology, spiritual ministry, and gerontology.

Strauss, William, and Neil Howe. *Generations: The History of America's Future 1584 to 2069*. New York: William Morrow & Co., 1991.

While each generation seems to have its own personality, Strauss and Howe come from generations of the same type. According to the authors, this book can bring new insight into the nature of each generation and anticipate the mood of decades to come. A good book for group study.

2 Special Focus on Issues of Racial Ethnic Older Persons

"I am about to do a new thing; now it springs forth,
do you not perceive it?"
Isaiah 43:19 (NRSV)

This priority issue addresses the need for interaction among the different cultures, in order to provide opportunity for the sharing of wisdom and concerns of older adults from different traditions. The rapid increase in the numbers of older Asians, Hispanics, African Americans, Native Americans, and others calls for the special focus of the church. The combination of age and racial minority make them particularly vulnerable to stress and deprivation, and care services are often difficult to find and when available are often less than adequate.

Racial-Ethnic Guidelines: A Resource for Pastors, Editors, Curriculum Writers and Others Engaged in Educational Ministries. Joint Educational Development. Printed by Frontier Press, Cumberland Presbyterian Church. This resource was developed by an ecumenical partnership and can be ordered through Alice Gantt, Congregational Ministries Division, 100 Witherspoon St., Louisville, KY 40202-1396. (502) 569-5477

A *Profile of Older Americans: 1998.* This brochure includes the latest statistics on older Americans in eleven key subject areas, including racial and ethnic composition. For up to ten free copies, write: AARP Fulfillment, 601 E Street, NW, Washington, DC 20049. An electronic version of this brochure may be accessed at http://www.aoa.dhhs.gov/aoa/stats/statpage.html.

Serving Elders of Color: Challenges to Providers and the Aging Network. American Society on Aging, 1992.

Individual copies may be ordered for $5.00 each. Bulk orders 5–10, $4.50; 11–25, $4.00; 25+, $3.50. Order from the American Society on Aging, 833 Market St., Suite 512, San Francisco, CA 94103. (415) 974-9600

Sotomayor, Marta. "Racial and Ethnic Concerns in Aging." Chapter 9 in *Older Adult Ministry: A Resource for Program Development.* Presbyterian Publishing House, 1987. Order #085429

Available from Presbyterian Distribution Service, 100 Witherspoon St., Louisville, KY 40202-1396. (800) 524-2612

This book is one of three basic manuals in Older Adult Ministry published by the Office of Older Adult Ministry. Information about the manuals is listed in this bibliography under Publications of the Presbyterian Church (U.S.A.). Topics included in the article mentioned here are "Who Are the Minority Older People?", "Issues Facing Minority Older Adults," "Informal

Helping Networks and Minority Older Adults,"
"Community Services and Minority Older Adults," and
"Specific Ways Congregations Can Help."

Jackson, James S., Linda M. Chatters, Robert Joseph
Taylor. *Aging in Black America.* Thousand Oaks, Calif.:
Sage Publications, 1993.

This well-written book examines the status and living
situations of black older adults from a perspective that
addresses their special circumstances and overall coping
capacity. Research is based on analysis of data from a
national survey of the black population.

Wimberly, Anne Streaty, ed. *Honoring African American
Elders: A Ministry in the Soul Community.* San Francisco:
Jossey-Bass Publishers, 1997.

Older adults are the fastest growing segment of the
African-American churchgoing population. This is the
first book written to examine the church's vital role in
the lives of these older persons, and the critical need to
prepare church leaders to respond effectively to their
increasing numbers in congregations. A new model for
ministry is presented based on "honor" and "soul community." While this book presents a scholarly approach
to the issues, it is also very practical in its application of
the model theories.

3   Health Care and
Housing Concerns

"Even though I walk through the valley of the shad-
ow of death, I fear no evil; for thou art with me; thy
rod and thy staff, they comfort me."
Psalm 23:4 (RSV)

This priority issue is designed to encourage churches to
foster and support a response to society's need for a health
care system that is affordable and accessible to everyone.
In addition, there is a focus on care for the caregivers of
older persons, and on assisting congregations in encouraging lifestyles and wellness programs that promote good
health and wholeness. Additionally, the congregation can
assure that a minimum standard of basic and necessary survival support systems are made available to all older
adults, regardless of living situation. Such support systems
can include adequate health resource systems, adult day-
care centers, and adequate housing arrangements that
meet the needs of older adults, and that are comprehensive, accessible, and feasible within available resources.

Kalicki, Anne C., and Ann Trueblood Raper, eds.
*National Continuing Care Directory: Retirement
Communities with Nursing Care.* 2d ed. *American
Association of Homes for the Aging.* Glenview, Ill.: Scott,

Foresman & Co., 1988. Published by AARP, Washington, D.C.

This is a good resource book for a Presbytery Resource Center to have on hand, especially for the sake of those who wish to explore this lifestyle option. The directory provides information about continuing care facilities across the nation that will enable individuals to make decisions about whether or not a facility meets their personal wants, needs, and budget.

Presbyterian Homes in the United States, 1998. Presbyterian Association of Homes for the Aging, 510 N. Brookside Dr., Little Rock, AR 72205. (501) 225-1615

This book gives a listing of all Presbyterian-related care facilities in the United States with information concerning the number of beds, units, or apartments, church affiliation, and location, addresses, administrators' names and telephone numbers.

Resolution on Christian Responsibility and a National Medical Plan. A report approved by the 203rd General Assembly (1991) of the PC(USA). Published by the Office of the General Assembly, 100 Witherspoon St., Louisville, KY, 40202-1396. Available for $1.50 each from Presbyterian Distribution Service (PDS), (800) 524-2612. Order #OGA-91-021

Scheller, Mary Dale. *Building Partnerships in Hospital Care: Empowering Patients, Families and Professionals.* Palo Alto, Calif.: Bull Publishing Co., 1988.

The author of this book sets forth the premise that

caring is a partnership among three players—the patient, the family member or friend, and the health professional. She believes this is a partnership that is not used to its fullest potential. By combining the strengths and talents of the three players, in cooperation with each other, she believes they can extend their effectiveness, heighten their creativity, spread their energy, and achieve small miracles. This book discusses how this can happen.

The Congregation: A Community of Care and Healing: Health and Wholeness Awareness Resources. Presbyterian Church (U.S.A.)/Presbyterian Health Network, 100 Witherspoon St., Louisville, KY 40202-1396. (502) 569-5793

This book is designed to help local leaders and congregations to understand and engage in ministry related to health. It is intended to be a first-step guide for the congregation to become a place for healing, promoting healthy lifestyles, and becoming a caring community.

Westberg, Granger E. *The Parish Nurse: Providing a Minister of Health for Your Congregation.* Minneapolis: Augsburg Fortress, 1990.

Growing numbers of churches are intentionally becoming centers for health care with a spiritual dimension. Congregations ask how they can help bring about a climate that promotes holistic living, how to give assistance in preventive medicine, and health education, and how to help motivate people to care for their own health. This book points to a way for accomplishing these things through the parish nurse model.

McKim, Donald K., ed. *God Never Forgets: Faith, Hope, and Alzheimer's Disease.* Louisville, Ky.: Westminster John Knox Press, 1997.

This book is a must for the pastor's desk, church libraries, resource centers, and in the homes of families who are affected by the devastation of Alzheimer's disease. The book offers practical and spiritual assistance, helping to seek and find God's presence in the midst of very difficult times. The different chapters were written by well-known authors such as Stephen Sapp, James Ellor, and Denise D. Hopkins.

Wiest, Walter E., ed. *Health Care and Its Costs: A Challenge for the Church.* Lanham, Md.: University Press of America, 1988.

This book consists of essays commissioned by the Task Force on Health Costs/Policies of the Presbyterian Church (U.S.A.). Section I deals with the facts of health care in America. Section II deals with ethical concepts and principles. Section III covers a variety of themes having to do with health, illness, and healing in the life and ministry of the church.

Anderson, Herbert, and Freda A. Gardner. *Living Alone.* Louisville, Ky.: Westminster John Knox Press, 1997.

This book can be of special help to those who seek to minister to persons who live alone, as well as to those persons who live alone, and those who care about them.

4 Education and Action concerning Abuse of Older Adults

"Do not cast me off in the time of old age;
do not forsake me when my strength is spent."
Psalm 71:9 (NRSV)

An increasingly important priority is the protection of older adults from neglect, abuse, and exploitation, whether physical, emotional, psychological, or economic, and whether resulting from families, care facilities, business firms, or society in general. The church is in a unique position to educate its members and staff concerning the signs of abuse, and to give support and guidance to families where abuse takes place, as well as to promote in the educational program of the church those behaviors that are nonviolent and nonabusive.

Horton, Anne, and Judith A. Williamson, eds. *Abuse and Religion: When Praying Isn't Enough*. Lexington, Mass.: Lexington Books, 1988.

In this book, experts on family violence, religious leaders, and members of abusive families offer practical "how-to" insights on this generally unacknowledged population of abused elderly. The book offers guidelines for identification and diagnosis, strategies for change, intervention, and treatment choices. Chapter 4, p. 29, deals directly with "Abuse of the Elderly in the Home."

Turner, Patricia Gill, ed., *Family Violence: A Religious Issue: A Study/Action Guide for Congregations.* 1988. Available from Presbyterian Distribution Service, 100 Witherspoon Street, Louisville, KY 40202, for $1.00. Order #28388001. (800) 524-2612. *The Family Violence Study Guide* is available from the same place as listed above for $1 each, and the order number is OGA-91-019.

Decalmer, Peter and Frank Glendenning, eds. *The Mistreatment of Elderly People.* London and Newbury Park, Calif.: Sage Publications, 1993.

This book opens up discussion and presents an overview of the key research and theoretical explanations of elder abuse. In a series of essays, the various contributions draw together the perspectives of professionals from different disciplines. The book argues for clearer explanations of abuse and goes beyond immediate practical considerations and observations, giving clear guidelines for tackling and preventing the problem.

5 Emphasis on Intergenerational Experiences

"He [your grandson] shall be to you a restorer of life
and a nourisher of your old age."
Ruth 4:15 (NRSV)

While traditionally the church has separated the ages, there is a great need for interaction and appreciation of persons from other generations. The church can provide opportunities for intergenerational learning, sharing of culture and tradition, wisdom gained from experience, fellowship, and worship. In a mobile society, where grandparents and grandchildren are sometimes separated by many miles, the church can provide "adopted" grandparents. In situations where grandparents are, in fact, parenting their grandchildren, the church can provide practical help and support to the grandparents.

Growing Together: An Intergenerational Sourcebook. American Association of Retired Persons, 1985. Available from AARP, 601 E St., NW, Washington, DC 20049.

Although this resource was published in 1985, it is filled with timeless ideas for intergenerational activities.

Side by Side. A musical production brings together older adult and young voices. Music and lyrics by Sheldon

Curry. Book by Doris Simpson. Published by Laurel Press, Sugarloaf Shores, Florida. Distributed by The Lorenz Corporation, 501 E. Third St., Box 802, Dayton, OH 45401.

This is a delightful musical production that discovers within its story the magic of combining youth and age, as the characters discover their special ability to understand and communicate with each other.

Newman, Sally, and Steven W. Brummel, eds., *Intergenerational Programming*. Binghamton, N.Y.: Haworth Press, 1992.

This is a very helpful, practical book, full of good ideas for developing intergenerational programs.

6   Spirituality and Aging

"But we have this treasure in earthen vessels, to
show that the transcendent power belongs to God
and not to us. We are afflicted in every way, but not
crushed; perplexed, but not driven to despair;
persecuted, but not forsaken; struck down, but not
destroyed; always carrying in the body the death of
Jesus, so that the life of Jesus may also be
manifested in our bodies."
2 Cor. 4:7–10 (RSV)

The spiritual needs of older persons resulting from the many
changes, transitions, and losses that accumulate and sometimes accelerate in the later years of life is the focus of this
priority issue. The spiritual needs of older people are basical-
ly the same as those of other age groups. However, the needs
may differ in intensity as well as in character. An important
concept in spiritual growth is that such growth does not nor-
mally happen in isolation. It involves a continuous process
of relationship and interdependence between God and the
self in the community of faith throughout all of life. The
need of older adults for continued faith growth experiences
must have the attention of the church, particularly as they
face accumulated losses, reflect on the life they have lived,
and seek meaning for the later years of life.

Bianchi, Eugene. *Aging as a Spiritual Journey*. New York: Crossroad, 1984.

A scholarly approach to aging as a spiritual journey, this book is recommended for those who wish to think deeply about the aging process, who wish to age more gracefully and creatively, and who are interested in a qualitative rather than a quantitative understanding of life from birth to death.

Hutchison, Frank. *Aging Comes of Age*. Louisville, Ky.: Westminster/John Knox Press, 1991.

This book gives encouragement to mature persons who wish to have satisfying personal lives while contributing to society. The author outlines many facets of a better and greatly expanded life by pointing out the many options available for the involvement of older persons.

Missinne, Leo E. *Reflections on Aging: A Spiritual Guide*, 1990. Liguori Publications, One Liguori Drive, Liguori, MO 63057-9999.

Written by a professor of gerontology at the University of Nebraska who is also an ordained Roman Catholic priest, this book reflects on some of the deepest questions of human existence in older age: What is life all about? What is the meaning of suffering? What is the purpose of living as a handicapped older person? How are we to understand our death and dying process? Is there a specific spirituality and theology of older age?

Morgan, Richard L. *No Wrinkles on the Soul*. Nashville: Upper Room Books, 1990.

A series of sixty-two meditations that can be used for individual or small group daily devotions. Each meditation also includes suggested scripture reading, a printed Bible verse, and a reading for reflection. In a sensitive and honest way, the author deals with the major issues faced by persons in the later years.

Morgan, Richard L. *I Never Found That Rocking Chair*. Nashville: Upper Room Books, 1993.

This delightful book reflects on questions about retirement such as When? What Shall I Do? Who Will I Be? Included are the author's reflections about his own retirement and these provide valuable insights for those looking toward retirement.

Morgan, Richard L. *From Grim to Green Pastures*. Nashville: Upper Room Books, 1994.

Another very helpful book by Morgan, this was written especially for persons experiencing health difficulties, and their caregivers. Useful for hospital chaplains and retirement home chaplains, as well as for patients or residents in care facilities.

Morgan, Richard L. *Autumn Wisdom*. Nashville: Upper Room Books, 1995.

This book is made up of older adults speaking for themselves. The stories are short and very readable, and are naturals for meditation and reflection, and for personal and small group devotions. It is also a very appropriate gift for an older person.

Morgan, Richard L. *Remembering Your Story: A Guide to Spiritual Autobiography*. Nashville: Upper Room Books, 1996.

Richard Morgan once again provides for group participation in this guide for assisting and encouraging groups of older persons, or individuals, to reach back into their histories and tell their stories. Those who read this book will learn to enjoy their life story, bring healing to past hurts, and remember the sacred moments in their lives. A leader's guide is also available to assist in the use of this book.

Morgan, Richard L. *With Faces to the Evening Sun.* Nashville: Upper Room Books, 1998.

These meditations written for nursing home residents and their families, trace the unrelenting rhythm of God's presence and amazing bursts of hope and humor, even amidst the sadness of change and loss. The author shares stories about life in the nursing home from the first strange days of settling in to the day it begins to feel like home. Each meditation contains suggested scripture reading, a printed Bible verse, and a closing prayer.

Nouwen, Henri J., and Walter Gaffney. *Aging: The Fulfillment of Life.* Garden City, N.Y.: Doubleday, 1986.

This book provides a valuable perspective on the potentials of age, the renewal of relations among the generations, and the ministry of caring as the way to self and to others.

Seeber, James J., ed. *Spiritual Maturity in the Later Years.* Binghamton, N.Y.: Haworth Press, 1990.

This is a compilation of essays by leaders in the field of religion and aging that address the important issue of spiritual growth and change during the aging process.

The approach is sensitive, balanced, and scholarly, and provides insights in an area that is long overdue. A must for professionals working with or relating to older adults.

Tournier, Paul. *Learn to Grow Old.* Louisville, Ky.: Westminster/John Knox Press, 1990.

A classic, published first in 1972, again in 1983, and now republished. In this warm, sensitive, fact-filled book, the author deals specifically with many aspects of aging—society's attitude, the quality of life, loneliness, and facing death. He believes we must all learn to grow old, and that the process is most successfully accomplished when we prepare and plan for it throughout life. This is a book for all ages.

Fischer, Kathleen. *Winter Grace.* New York: Paulist Press, 1985.

This book is a must for anyone interested in spirituality in the later years. *Winter Grace* describes spirituality not as a separate compartment of life, but as the deepest dimension of all experience. The main theme is that the losses accompanying the aging process can lead to freedom and new life.

Fischer, Kathleen. *Autumn Gospel.* New York: Paulist Press, 1995.

This popular author explores the spiritual dimensions of women's middle and later years by weaving together stories, experiences, and research from a variety of traditions and cultures. The book presents the central image of later life as autumn.

Simmons, Henry C. *In the Footsteps of the Mystics: A Guide to the Spiritual Classics*. New York: Paulist Press, 1992.

In this book, the author offers help in coming to know the spiritual mentors of the ages. First, he offers a simple personality profile of four "ways" of spirituality. Then, he gathers together short excerpts from a variety of classic spiritual writers. The reader is invited to "come, meet and talk with" the women and men who, across the centuries, have come to know God intimately.

Simmons, Henry C., and Mark A. Peters. *With God's Oldest Friends*. New York: Paulist Press, 1996.

This is a very practical and helpful book, especially useful for pastors and members of visitation committees visiting older persons who are homebound or in nursing homes. There is an art to such visitations and this book is an excellent guidebook for this important ministry.

Brandt, Leslie. *Bible Readings for Troubled Times*. Minneapolis: Augsburg Publishing House, 1984.

This devotional book is designed to help make and maintain the spiritual connections in the midst of trouble and suffering. Each one-page reflection includes scripture readings, a meditation, a prayer, and a question or statement to ponder. While the author makes no attempt to answer the problem of pain, he talks of God's concern and love for human beings despite the troubles that afflict their lives.

Thibault, Jane Marie. *A Deepening Love Affair: The Gift of God in Later Life*. Nashville: Upper Room Books, 1993.

This book is for older persons who seek to enrich their spiritual lives. Dr. Thibault is a clinical gerontologist, and states that she has written this book for the "mature adult who is spiritually discontented" and who sees that as a positive experience and opportunity for growth.

Kimble, Melvin A.; Susan H. McFadden, James W. Ellor, and James J. Seeber, eds. *Aging, Spirituality and Religion: A Handbook*. Minneapolis: Augsburg Fortress Press, 1995.

This book examines the ways religion and spirituality are experienced by older persons within a society of older adults. Its aim is to encompass the wholeness of the older person's life, including spiritual yearnings that are often shaped by religious faith and practice. Contributors from a variety of disciplines explore this theme. This book can serve as an important tool in studying in the areas of health care, psychology, spiritual ministry, and gerontology.

Carl, William J., Jr., ed. *Graying Gracefully: Preaching to Older Adults*. Louisville, Ky.: Westminster John Knox Press, 1997.

This book gives practical examples of biblical and theological sermons for the older members of the congregation, and perhaps for all ages, helping the pastor to proclaim the Good News effectively to older adults. It covers topics from biblical and historical views of aging, to matters of social justice. Each chapter gives helpful suggestions as well as a sermon to illustrate the issues discussed.

7 Global and Ecumenical Older Adult Concerns

"Thus says the Lord: Stand by the roads, and look, and ask for the ancient paths, where the good way is; and walk in it, and find rest for your souls."

Jeremiah 6:16 (RSV)

Addressing the issues of aging as a global phenomenon, this priority issue encourages the exchange of expertise, wisdom, experience, and resources among nations and faiths around the world, bringing together models for meeting the needs of older persons and using wisdom and skills that reach beyond the Presbyterian Church (U.S.A.) and beyond the United States.

Global Aging: Comparative Indicators and Future Trends. U.S. Department of Commerce, 1991. Economics and Statistics Administration, Bureau of the Census, Washington, DC 20233.

Summary Report. World Council of Churches Consultation, Ministry with Senior Citizens, 1991.

This paper presents the issues discussed at the consultation and contains recommendations for action for older adults, congregations, and international organizations. Available free from the Office of Older Adult

Ministry, Room 1516, 100 Witherspoon St., Louisville, KY 40202-1396. (502) 569-5487

Paul, Susanne S., and James A. Paul. *Humanity Comes of Age*. Geneva, Switzerland: Risk Book Series, WCC Publications 1994.

This informative and fact-filled book was a result of the consultation on "Ministry with Senior Citizens" held in October 1991 which was convened by the World Council of Churches' sub-unit on Renewal and Congregational Life. It explores most of the familiar issues that we deal with in the United States, but with a global dimension to each issue, and needs to be on the shelf of each church library.

Global Aging Report. News digest published six times a year by AARP, 601 E Street, NW, Washington, DC 20049. $40 for one-year subscription. $20 for seniors and students. 1-800-424-3410

This is a bimonthly roundup of news about aging worldwide.

Sokolovsky, Jay, ed. *The Cultural Context of Aging: Worldwide Perspectives*. New York: Bergin & Garvey Publishers, 1990.

A collection of specially commissioned articles, this significant book focuses on the multitude of cultural solutions that societies worldwide have available for dealing with the challenges, problems, and opportunities of growing old.

8 Congregational Ministry with Older Adults

"So even to old age and gray hairs, O God, do not forsake me, till I proclaim thy might to all the generations to come. Thy power and thy righteousness, O God, reach the high heavens."
*Psalm 71:18–19 (*RSV*)*

Presbyterian Church (U.S.A.) Publications
The Presbyterian Church (U.S.A.) has published many helpful resources as aids to congregations who wish to begin or to enhance their older adult ministry program. Many of these are in your presbytery resource center. If you wish to order your own copy, they are available through Presbyterian Distribution Service.

Abundant Life for Aging People: Our Vision and Our Calling. Order from Presbyterian Distribution Service, 100 Witherspoon St., Louisville, KY 40202-1396. Order #21785423. (800) 524-2612

A statement of the 193rd General Assembly (1981) of the United Presbyterian Church U.S.A. Includes recommended strategies and survey findings.

Ministry with Aging. Order from Presbyterian Distribution Service, 100 Witherspoon St., Louisville, KY 40202-1396. Order #21785422.

A statement of the 119th General Assembly (1979) of the Presbyterian Church U.S.

The Rights and Responsibilities of Older Persons. Order from Presbyterian Distribution Service, 100 Witherspoon St., Louisville, KY 40202-1396. Order #21785428.

A statement of the 185th General Assembly (1973) of the United Presbyterian Church.

Older Adult Ministry: A Resource for Program Development. Order from Presbyterian Distribution Service, 100 Witherspoon St., Louisville, KY 40202-1396. Order #21785429.

Published in 1987, this helpful manual provides strategies, program plans, and theological reflections for churches seeking resources for older adult ministry.

Older Adult Ministry: A Guide for the Presbytery Committee. Written by Jack and Sue Angerman. Order from Presbyterian Distribution Service, 100 Witherspoon St., Louisville, KY 40202-1396. Order #18090300.

Published in 1990, this manual is designed to help presbyteries initiate ministries with older adults. It outlines ways in which the church can translate concern into action.

Older Adult Ministry: A Guide for the Session and Congregation. Written by Jim Simpson and edited by Kim Richter. Order from Presbyterian Distribution Service, 100 Witherspoon St., Louisville, KY 40202-1396. Order #18090301.

This manual is designed to help the local congregation initiate ministry with older adults. It is a compilation of successful programs and strategies resulting from the Gift of a Lifetime project. It contains a study guide for exploring the issues of aging based on material found in *Older Adult Ministry: A Resource for Program Development,* listed above.

Older Adult Ministry: Growing in the Abundant Life. Report of the Task Force on Older Adult Ministry at the 1992 General Assembly. Available from Presbyterian Distribution Service, 100 Witherspoon St., Louisville, KY 40202-1396. Order # OGA-92-018. (800) 524-2612

This book sets forth the seven priority issues to be addressed by the church in the next decade, with strategies suggested for each area of the church. This book is designed to raise awareness and to educate the church concerning the issues of older adults, and to encourage developing a ministry that serves the needs and uses the gifts of older adult members.

AGEnda. Available through the Congregational Ministries Division, Room 1516, 100 Witherspoon St., Louisville, KY 40202-1396. (502) 569-5487. Free upon request.

A quarterly update on news, program ideas, worship materials, and helpful resources for ministry with older adults.

Older Adult Ministry: Growing in the Abundant Life. Church papers: Short-term study course for adults. Available through Presbyterian Distribution Service, 100 Witherspoon St., Louisville, KY 40202-1396. Order # 042100.

This book was written by Starr Luteri and edited by Frank Hainer, associate for adult education and curriculum development for the Presbyterian Church (U.S.A.). The book is based on the Report of the Task Force to the General Assembly in 1992. It provides an opportunity to study the demographics of current society, and how the church might address the increasing numbers of older adults in our congregations.

Aging Is a Family Affair. Written by Ed Loper. Published by Presbyterian Mariners. Order from Carolyn and Larry Gabbard, 11555 West 78th Drive, Arvada, CO 80005-3427. (303) 225-5033

Ed Loper writes especially for the adult children of parents who may, in their later years, look to their children for support and help. However, many of those called upon for assistance do not feel equipped emotionally or spiritually for the responsibility. This book can serve as a study guide in exploring the issues involved and seeking ways to keep it all together.

Adult Children Caring for Their Parents: A Training Design. Written by John Rhea. Available through Presbyterian Distribution Service, 100 Witherspoon St., Louisville, KY 40202-1396. Order # 70-250-96-706. (800) 524-2612

This book is produced for the use of synod, presbytery, and congregational events, conferences, retreats, and for other purposes that result in assisting adult children caring for their parents and other family members. It was originally published in 1983 by the Office on Aging, Presbyterian Church U.S., Atlanta, Ga., and has been updated, edited, and republished by the Office of Older Adult Ministry, Louisville, Ky.

Older Adult Week Planning Packet. Order from Presbyterian Distribution Service, 100 Witherspoon St., Louisville, KY 40202-1396. (800) 524-2612. Free upon request.

The first week in May each year on the church planning calendar is designated as Older Adult Week. The purpose for having an Older Adult Week is to honor aging, and to recognize and honor the older members of the congregation. The focus of Older Adult Week is to encourage the view that aging is a natural part of living, involving the entire life span from birth to death, and to affirm and celebrate aging for all ages. This packet is designed to assist congregations in building programs to celebrate Older Adult Week, identifying both the unique needs and the special gifts and skills of older adults, seeking ways to address their needs and use their skills.

Two Videos

1. *Aging Me . . . Aging You . . . The Journey of a Lifetime.* A VHS video produced in 1994 by the Media Services Team and the Office of Older Adult Ministry of the Presbyterian Church (U.S.A.). Available from Presbyterian Distribution Service, 100 Witherspoon St., Louisville, KY 40202-1396. $19.95 plus postage. Order # 70250-94-704. (800) 524-2612

This new video is for general audiences, giving a glimpse into the journey called "aging," seen as an adventure that begins with the beginning of life and continues throughout life. It presents aging in a realistic manner, including the upside and the downside of the aging process, and suggests models for ministry with older persons. A study guide comes with the video.

2. *Aging Me . . . Aging You . . . Exploring the Issues.* Produced in 1995 by Media Services Team and the Office on Older Adult Ministry of the Presbyterian Church (U.S.A.), this video is available from Presbyterian Distribution Service, 100 Witherspoon St., Louisville, KY 40202-1396. $19.95 plus postage. Order # 70250-95-705. (800) 524-2612

A companion video to the one listed above, this is a study video designed to start discussions around five issues: ageism, death and dying, spirituality and aging, care for the caregiver, and justice. An extensive study guide that provides guidance in leading discussions on these five segments of the video is available for free.

Other Publications

Some of the classics that have been published during the last two decades have good ideas and doable suggestions for beginning and maintaining an older adult ministry in your congregation.

Becker, Arthur H. *Ministry with Older Persons: A Guide for Clergy and Congregations.* Minneapolis: Augsburg Publishing House, 1986.

This book provides basic information necessary for understanding the aging process and older people, as well as including practical guidance on developing effective ministry with older adults. It deals with how congregations might respond to the needs of increasing numbers of older persons, as well as how to enable the older persons to use their many gifts in ministry.

Vogel, Linda Jane. *The Religious Education of Older Adults*. Birmingham, Ala.: Religious Education Press, 1984.
   A helpful resource for persons engaged in planning and implementing teaching-learning opportunities with older persons. The author weaves the psychological, sociological, educational, and religious experiences that impact the later years into opportunities present in the church's education ministry with older adults.

Tilberg, Cedric W. *Revolution Underway: An Aging Church in an Aging Society*. Philadelphia: Fortress Press, 1984.
   The author maintains that the aging of society is not only a societal issue, but that the church must take responsibility for addressing and coping with the problems that aging brings about. Tilberg calls on the church to revolutionize its outlook, and to respond in a new and creative fashion to the force of the demographic transition now in progress.

Robb, Thomas B. *Growing Up: Pastoral Nurture for the Later Years*. Binghamton, N.Y.: Haworth Press, 1991.
   This is a helpful book for all those who work with and care about older adults. Taking into account the findings of developmental research, it moves further to the more personal, spiritual dimensions of growing up and growing old. The book includes advice and practical programs for enabling older adults to retain their status as meaningful members of their congregations and communities.

Arn, Win, and Charles Arn. *Catch the Age Wave*. Grand Rapids: Baker Book House, 1994.

This book is for helping congregations respond to the rapidly growing population of older adults. Discussed are specific ways churches can establish ministries to reach the diverse needs of older adults, combating the myths and fostering a new appreciation for this age group.

Gentzler, Richard H., Jr., and Donald F. Clingan. *Aging: God's Challenge to Church and Synagogue*. Discipleship Resources, P.O. Box 840, Nashville, TN 37202.

This new resource from the United Methodist Church and the Christian Church (Disciples of Christ) presents an unbelievable amount of information, program ideas, resources, procedures, and supportive encouragement for persons engaged in or planning for older adult ministry. It is clear, organized, and filled with practical solutions for the challenge of responding to the needs of increasing numbers of older persons.

Carlson, Dosia. *Engaging in Ministry with Older Adults*. Alban Institute, 1997.

The author did research among mainline denominations to determine where significant ministries for older people were being done. With the results of this research, she produced a rare resource for congregations who are seeking help in designing and implementing programs for, with, and by older adults. The book is a joy to read, reflecting the ever-present wit of the author.

9   The Bible and Aging

"Honor your father and your mother, as the Lord your
God commanded you, so that your days may be long
and that is may go well with you in the land that the
Lord your God is giving you."
Deut. 5:16 (NRSV)

"For old age is not honored for length of time, or mea-
sured by number of years; but understanding is gray hair
for anyone, and a blameless life is ripe old age."
Wisdom of Solomon 4:8–9 (NRSV)

Perhaps as a part of your focus on older adult ministry, you
would like to do a study of aging in the Bible. The following books are suggested:

Stagg, Frank. *The Bible Speaks on Aging*. Nashville:
Broadman Press, 1981.

A thorough study of the scriptures in the Old
Testament and the New Testament relative to the aging
process, this book is appreciated by both scholars and
laypersons. It is concerned with helping older people
understand themselves better, and helping younger people understand older people better and relate to them
more compassionately.

Harris, J. Gordon. *Biblical Perspectives on Aging: God and the Elderly*. Philadelphia: Fortress Press, 1987.

Deeply rooted in critical study, this book offers an amazing amount of fresh historical-critical data. It studies present-day social settings where, while people are living longer, the old social networks of human care and valuing are becoming less and less effective.

Sapp, Stephen. *Full of Years: Aging and the Elderly in the Bible and Today*. Nashville: Abingdon Press, 1987.

In this writing, the author deals in a very scholarly way with the multiple aspects of growing old. Included are contemporary issues, aging in the Old Testament and the New Testament, attitudes toward aging, and obligations toward older persons.

10 Caring for Older Relatives

"When you were young, you girded yourself and walked
where you would; but when you are old, you will
stretch out your hands, and another will guide you and
carry you where you do not wish to go."
John 21:18 (RSV)

Caregiving for older relatives is a fast-growing phenomenon and one that many families do not anticipate. Therefore, families often come into these responsibilities without the needed knowledge and understanding. These books may be helpful:

Hooyman, Nancy R., and Wendy Lustbader. *Taking Care: Supporting Older People and Their Families.* New York: Free Press, 1986.

This book includes an explanation of the physical, mental, and emotional changes associated with aging, and offers practical solutions to the dilemmas faced by caregiving families, especially by women caught in the middle between caring for children and parents, and maintaining responsibilities at the workplace. It includes good information about community resources, assistance programs, ready-to-use charts, information sheets, and checklists.

Silverstone, Barbara, and Helen Kandel Hyman. *You and Your Aging Parent*. 3d ed. New York: Pantheon Books, 1989.

Originally published in 1976, this book is now regarded as one of the first to recognize that the problems of older persons could not be considered without understanding the needs of their middle-aged children. Completely updated and extensively revised, this edition focuses on the impact of important changes and developments affecting the condition of older persons and their care.

Shelley, Florence D. *When Your Parents Grow Old*. New York: Harper & Row, Publishers, 1988.

If you are caring for your mother or father, there is invaluable information in this book to help you. It includes information on finding help in the community, improving the quality of the parent's life, housing concerns, home care and nursing home care, money matters, doctors, hospitals and HMOs, diseases and disorders of older persons, successful aging, and agencies and organizations that can help. This is a very practical, sensible, and informative resource.

Sullender, R. Scott. *Losses in Later Life*. New York: Paulist Press, 1989.

This book discusses the major and unique aspects of losses that take place in later life. It is a good resource for pastors, retirement community chaplains, persons caring for their parents, and others working with older persons. The author seeks to describe "a new way of walking with God" by learning to grieve over losses and moving on to new identities and new spiritual meanings that were not possible to discover earlier in the life span.

Bridges, William. *Transitions: Making Sense of Life's Changes.* Reading, Mass.: Addison-Wesley Publishing Co., 1980.

This book helps both in identifying and in coping with the critical changes in life, taking the reader step by step through the transition process, and offering skills, suggestions, and advice for negotiating through endings, in-between times, and new beginnings.

Manning, Doug. *When Love Gets Tough: The Nursing Home Dilemma.* San Francisco: Harper & Row, Publishers, 1990.

This book is especially helpful for adult children who anticipate moving a parent into a nursing home, or for the parent who will live there. It is a very caring, warm, and   realistic approach to what is many times a very painful transition. The chapters address such issues as: "Making the Decision," "Implementing the Decision," "Adjusting to the Decision," and "Living with the Decision."

Rushford, Patricia H. *Caring for Your Elderly Parents.* Grand Rapids: Fleming H. Revell (a division of Baker Book House), 1993.

A very practical book for helping to deal with the many challenges that come with caring for elderly family members. The author dispels the myths and fears about aging and equips the reader for the task of caring for elderly parents by addressing subjects such as living arrangements, finances, home care, illnesses, and medical help.

11   Books on Retirement

"Even to your old age and gray hairs, I am he, I am he
who will sustain you. I have made you and I will carry
you; I will sustain you and I will rescue you."
Isaiah 46:4 (NIV)

Retirement is a comparatively new concept. Up until very recent times, persons might work until they were sixty-five, then retire, live a couple of years, and die. However, currently, with the life expectancy nearing eighty, many older persons live twenty and sometimes twenty-five years past their retirement age. The big question is: How does the retired person find meaning and fulfillment for life during those remaining years? Here are some suggested helpful books:

Gross, Deborah. *Beyond the Gold Watch*. Louisville, Ky.: Westminster John Knox Press, 1994.

   The author addresses many important retirement issues in this book, including decisions to be made, and planning for retirement. There are worksheets provided to help the reader fit the suggestions to his or her own unique circumstances.

Kuhn, Maggie. *No Stone Unturned: The Life and Times of Maggie Kuhn*. New York: Ballantine Books, 1991.

In this book, Maggie Kuhn tells the story of her remarkable life—of independent womanhood, of the importance of having goals larger than ourselves, and of growing old with dignity. This is delightful reading about an outstanding woman committed to the politics of aging. It is good reading for all ages.

Maitland, David J. *Aging as Counterculture: A Vocation for the Later Years*. New York: Pilgrim Press, 1991.

This book describes the need for older adults to defy the American culture's obsession with youth through positive action and life-affirming activities. It urges readers to find ways of refuting the current societal message that "old" means "no longer viable." Aging is presented as a time of life that has unique features that are as attractive as those of life's earlier stages.

Sapp, Stephen. *Light on a Gray Area: American Public Policy on Aging*. Nashville: Abingdon Press, 1992.

In this significant book, Dr. Sapp views public policy implications on "the graying of America" from the viewpoint of Christian theological ethics, placing special emphasis on the importance of interdependence among the generations.

Friedan, Betty. *The Fountain of Age*. New York: Simon & Schuster, 1993.

In 1963 Friedan wrote *The Feminine Mystique*, changing the way women thought about themselves and the way society thought about women. In 1993 she wrote this book about aging. She seeks to change the way all of us, both men and women, think about ourselves as we grow older and the way society thinks about aging.

Sheehy, Gail. *New Passages: Mapping Your Life across Time*. New York: Random House, 1995.

In this new book, the author talks about the advent of a second adulthood after age forty-five. Rather than seeing the aging process after forty-five as decline and something to be denied and covered up, she encourages those approaching what she calls "middlescence" to regroup and prepare for the second adulthood in much the same way that we prepared for our first adulthood.

Raines, Robert. *A Time to Live: Seven Tasks of Creative Aging*. New York: Dutton, 1997.

In this very practical and helpful book, the author deals with important issues related to aging in healthy, positive, and creative ways. The tasks include "Embracing Sorrow," "Savoring Blessedness," "Re-imagining Work," "Nurturing Intimacy," "Seeking Forgiveness," and "Taking On the Mystery." Although the book deals with concrete problems, it is not simply a "maintenance manual." As the cover states, "It reflects a biblical spirituality that is non-sectarian and deeply human . . . rooted in down-to-earth living." A good group-study book.

Seymour, Robert E. *Aging without Apology: Living the Senior Years with Integrity and Faith*. Valley Forge, Pa.: Judson Press, 1995.

This is helpful reading for those looking toward

retirement soon, or for those who have just retired. The book deals with the many unexpected facets of retirement confronting most retirees. The topics include: "Coming to Terms with Your Self-Image," "Experiencing Retirement as a Religious Crisis," "Questioning Assumptions about Spirituality and Aging," Developing an Agenda for Healthy Aging," "Coping with Change," "Avoiding an Obsession with Health," and many others.

Saussy, Carroll. *The Art of Growing Old: A Guide to Faithful Aging*. Minneapolis: Augsburg, 1998.

This is an excellent book for group study. It has a scholarly approach to issues of aging, but at the same time suggests very practical ways of addressing them. The writing style is challenging and realistic, while evoking a positive attitude toward aging in the reader. The reflection questions are on target, and very helpful. This one is a must.

12 Videos

A number of videos made available by a variety of sources are listed for your perusal and use if they fit your particular needs.

Up Golden Creek. A color videocassette produced by the Office on Aging in Atlanta, Georgia, in the mid-1980s.

This video depicts the social and economic situation of older people and the growing tension over the rising cost of service and benefits to older persons. Available from presbytery resource centers.

Elder Abuse: Five Case Studies. Produced by Terra Nova Films, Inc., 9848 S. Winchester Avenue, Chicago, IL 60643. Directed by James Vanden Bosch. Purchase $195; Rental $55. Length: 40 minutes.

This film explores the issue of elder abuse from the points of view of five different persons living in abusive situations.

Changing Relationships. Produced by Terra Nova Films, Inc. 9848 S. Winchester Avenue, Chicago, IL 60643. Purchase $39.95; No rental. Length: 33 minutes.

In this video Dr. Martin Marty, Professor of Modern Christianity at the University of Chicago Divinity

School, talks about spirituality and religious faith as the context within which congregations deal with questions of aging. He also discusses the need for change among institutions, including the church, that are faced with the challenges associated with aging.

Older Adult Ministry at South Highland Presbyterian Church. Available on loan through the Presbyterian Older Adult Ministry Office, 100 Witherspoon St., Louisville, KY 40202-1396. Length: 14 minutes, 44 seconds.

This video presents a model of older adult ministry in a large downtown church (935 members, 350 over age fifty-five). Produced by South Highland Presbyterian Church, Birmingham, Alabama, as a part of the Gift of a Lifetime Project of the Presbyterian Church (U.S.A.). Involvement of older adults is portrayed in the description of the program carried out by this particular church.

Whisper: The Women. Order from Terra Nova Films, 9848 S. Winchester Avenue, Chicago, IL 60643. Purchase $89; Rental $35.

This short video presents seven older women of varied races and cultures relating simply but poignantly what aging means for them.

A Late Frost: Reflections on Aging. Order from Sunmark Productions, 8100 Penn Avenue South, Suite 150-B, Minneapolis MN 55431. Purchase $39.95, plus $3.00 mailing and handling. Length: 50 minutes.

This video uses interviews with children, older men and women, and the writings of the late Gerhard Frost to focus on what it feels like to grow old. It has 10 segments of about 5 minutes each, and the format allows for discussion after viewing each of the segments.

Congregations Who Care: The Ministry of Health and Wholeness. Order from Presbyterian Distribution Service, 100 Witherspoon St., Louisville KY 40202-1396. Order #72-660-94-004. Length: 25 minutes, 35 seconds.

This video presents ways that congregations can become involved in a ministry of health and wholeness. Included is a model of the parish nurse on the staff of a church who educates for and promotes healthy lifestyles among the members, teaches preventive medicine, and monitors the health of the members of the congregations.

Facing Death: A Two-Tape Series. Order from FEPI/Family Experiences Productions, Inc. P.O. Box 5879, Austin, TX 78763-5879.

Tape 1: Provides physical, emotional, and spiritual comfort to loved ones. This tape is designed to help terminally ill patients and their caregivers to "know what to expect" and how to comfort each other physically, emotionally, and spiritually. Length: 33 minutes.

Tape 2: Provides practical planning and discusses legal issues. This tape presents an exceptional nurse/attorney who explains the various legal instruments (wills, living wills, and other advance directives, including DNR Order and Durable Power of Attorney for Health Care) that can help patients get what they want. Legal issues confronting patients, their caregivers, and medical providers are discussed. Other topics covered include organ donation, bills and insurance, and funeral planning. Length: 30 minutes.

These videos are extremely helpful and sensitive as they share the thoughts, experiences, and suggestions of highly articulate and caring patients, caregivers, hospice professionals, physicians, and social workers.

Aging Parents: The Family Survival Guide. Order from: Livetapes Communications, Inc. 258 Howth Street, San Francisco, CA 94112-2416. (415) 333-0466.

Aging Parents was specifically designed to help anyone who does not know what to do or where to go for help, who needs information quickly but cannot afford expert counsel, who needs reference and referral sources for changing conditions, who wants to do short-term, inter- mediate, or long-range planning, or who needs a fresh perspective on his or her own situation. It offers solid information, advice, and perspective on the issues con- fronting families with aging parents who are increasingly in need of help.

Appendix A
Suggested Program Ideas

At some point in planning, when all the resources have been gathered, read, pondered, and chosen, it is necessary to translate all those ideas into programming. In an effort to get the creative juices flowing, some program ideas are shared here for each of the seven priority issues introduced in the listings of resources.

1. *Education and Leader Development*
   A. Plan a series of 4–5 weeks in the church educational program to study the aging process for all ages, identifying the changes and the needs inherent in each stage of growth. This series in the church school could follow or precede a weeklong emphasis involving the whole church during Older Adult Week in May.
   B. This plan could be expanded to include an educational experience for the various committees of the session, such as:

   1. Pastoral committees. Include training in the do's and don'ts of visiting the homebound and those members in nursing homes, how to detect signs of abuse, and information concerning available community services.

   2. Worship committees. Include raising the awareness of the committee concerning the importance of including older adult issues in the prayers, liturgies, and sermons in the Sunday morning worship services.

   3. Building and grounds committees. Assure that the church building is totally wheelchair and walker accessible, including restrooms, choir area, and pulpit.

   4. Stewardship committees. Provide opportunities for older members at all functioning levels to give of their time, talents, and money to the community of faith.

C. For leader development in older adult ministry, include annually the plan to   send appropriate persons to training conferences, such as the Annual Conference of the Presbyterian Older Adult Ministry Network (contact the Office of Older Adult Ministry at (502) 569-5487), and the Annual Skills for Older Adult Ministry Conference at Montreat Conference Center, Montreat, North Carolina, in May each year.

2. Special Focus on Issues of Racial Ethnic Older Persons

A. Identify needs in the community that are not being met, and work together with all congregations, including minority congregations, in planning community-wide programs that address the needs and use the wisdom and skills of the whole community together.

B. Invite speakers from other cultures to share at luncheons, from the pulpit, or through informal discussions on how their culture views older persons, how older persons of that culture live in their later years, and how they view the American system of care of older persons.

C. Plan an annual community-wide worship in celebration of aging for all ages, recognizing older persons who have made major contributions to the quality of life, especially the spiritual life, of the community.

3. Attention to Health Care and Housing Concerns

A. Consider the possibility of seeking a parish nurse to serve on the staff of the congregation to monitor the health of the members of the congregation, including especially the homebound and those in nursing homes; to develop an educational program for the entire congregation promoting good health practices of exercise, nutrition, and healthy handling of stress; and to teach the nonviolent management of conflict and anger. If this is not possible, set up a committee of the church made up of medical professionals who would be willing to serve in these areas.

B. Make a list of the care facilities, nursing homes, and retirement communities within a 50-mile radius of the church, and include services offered, restrictions on entering, costs, and so forth, so that when families reach crisis time, they will not need to start from square one in finding a place.

C. Have available in the church office a listing of services offered in the community for older persons, such as the Area Agency on Aging Services, Home Health Care Services, and Emergency Clinics, so that these "best kept secrets" can be used by those who need them.

D. Plan a series of programs in the adult church school to study issues of death and dying, including legal issues, medical ethics issues, living wills, and durable powers of attorney for health. Invite a lawyer, a medical doctor, a minister, and a social worker to make presentations and lead discussions. When the series is completed, plan a time following the morning worship service when people can prepare and sign their living wills and other papers related to dying with dignity. Have present a lawyer, a notary public, all the forms necessary, and a medical doctor to assist in understanding the forms.

4. *Education and Action concerning Abuse of Older Adults*

A. Plan an annual study retreat for the visitation and pastoral committees of the congregation, including the pastor, to discuss the issues of abuse. Include issues such as identifying the signs of abuse of older persons, what to do if you suspect but cannot prove abuse, and handling the dilemma that develops if the only caregiver of an older person is the abuser.

B. Be informed of the state laws concerning issues of abuse of older adults, so that if abuse is discovered, the person (or committee) knows what action to take.

C. Plan special classes in the church school on nonabusive behaviors.

5. *Emphasis on Intergenerational Experiences*

A. Assign children without grandparents nearby to older adults in the church who have no family nearby, to swap birthday gifts, visits, and telephone calls.

B. Develop a mentoring program of older adults helping young children and teenagers with their schoolwork as needed. At the same time, develop a mentoring program in which teenagers can help older adults with modern technologies such as computers and VCRs.

C. Plan a monthlong study series in the church school that provides for intergenerational Bible study and sharing of stories. Or match up church school classes intergenerationally for a month, to study, pray, and/or play together.

6. *Spirituality and Aging*

A. Plan events that recognize passages, achievements, transitions, and movements in the life of older persons, including anniversaries of the loss of a spouse, leaving the old home place, learning to walk again after a broken hip, and birthdays.

B. Lead groups of older persons in remembering their life stories, looking back in order to value their lives so far, and in integrating their pasts into their futures as they find new identities as older persons.

C. Plan a series of study opportunities for older persons in spiritual formation in order to enhance their continued spiritual growth through their later years. Carry these study opportunities into the homes of the homebound and into the nursing home when feasible.

7. *Global and Ecumenical Older Adult Concerns*

A. As members of the congregation travel overseas, give them the assignment of asking questions about the lives of older persons in the country visited. How do they live? How are they viewed? How are they cared for if they can no longer care for themselves? Then, ask for a report to be presented at some event upon the members' return.

B. Invite persons from other nations who are visiting or living temporarily in your community to form a panel to exchange ideas concerning aging, death and dying, living in the later years, and spirituality and aging among the different religions. Ask the panel to present a program at some event of the congregation.

Appendix B
"For the Gift of Length of Days"
A Hymn by Jane Parker Huber

For the gift of length of days
To be singing words of praise;
For the wisdom gained from years
Filled with work and joys and tears:

[Refrain]
Hear the thanks of youth and age
For our priceless heritage

For the eagerness of youth,
Searching for eternal truth;
For the willingness to learn
How to think and to discern:
[Refrain]

For the wish to sense and know,
And for children's urge to grow;
For their energy and zest,
Striving toward their very best:
[Refrain]

For the crowning gifts of age,
Love to share, thoughts to engage,
New perspectives still to learn,
New relationships to earn:
[Refrain]

For the freedom given to all
To respond to Christ's clear call,
Showing what must still be done
Here on earth to make us one:
[Refrain]

Jane Parker Huber, 1997
Dix, 7.7.7.7.7.7
Conrad Kocher, 1838
["For the Beauty of the Earth"]

Appendix C
"A Celebration of Age"
Model for a Worship Service

(This service of worship celebrating aging for all ages was developed by
Richard L. Morgan and is for congregational use as is, or to adapt as needed.)

"Rise in the presence of the aged. Show respect for the elderly
and revere your God." Leviticus 19:32 (NIV)

PRELUDE

WELCOME AND INTRODUCTIONS

CALL TO WORSHIP

Leader:	Aging is the human condition from the moment of our birth.
People:	Each stage holds a mixture of joy and sorrow, pain and mirth.
All:	Let us worship the God of all.
Leader:	People from all of life stages young and old, weak and strong.
People:	Claim the eternal Rock of Ages in whose love all belong.
All:	Let us worship the God of all.

Hymn: "We Gather Together" (Old Netherlands hymn)

PRAYER OF THANKSGIVING

O God, who has written in your eternal Word, "For everything,
there is a season, and a time for every activity under heaven":
we praise you for all seasons of life;

For the springtime, when life bursts forth in newness and joy, for the innocence of little children at Easter, their incessant probing questions and the awkward honesty of teenagers;

For the summer, with its relentless energy, driving adults to endless achievements and good works, for the warmth of maturing relationships, and the assurance that in the midst of life there is an invincible summer;

For the autumn, when life slows down and strength begins to depart and our feverish rush is tempered by the need to rest and reflect; for its golden richness which speaks of the mellowness and kindly wisdom of older people;

For the winter, when often all we can do is wait, while snow lies on top of the land, always aware that you are preparing the strong light and warm winds that lead to spring; when we realize that life's end is never far away, and yet there is always hope for the Resurrection Morning.

A MEDLEY OF OLD-TIME SONGS
HONORING OUR SPIRITUAL ELDERS

SOLO: "God of the Sparrow"

SCRIPTURE: Joshua 14:6–14; 2 Corinthians 4:7–18

SOLO: "The Lord's Prayer" by Klas Pieter

SERMON: "Celebrate Being Wisdom People"

*STATEMENT OF FAITH (unison)

We believe in the God of the First Age, who is present in the lives of little children and youth; who gives to every person the right to grow "in wisdom and in years, and in divine and human favor" (*Luke 2:52*, NRSV);

We believe in the God of the Second Age, who energizes young adults to find and realize their destiny in life; who sustains parents of children and youth; who invigorates those in mid-life; who gives to every person the right to grow "in wisdom and years" and in divine and human favor;

We believe in the God of the Third Age, who stands with those who retire from work, granting them peace, and nudging them to creative new beginnings; who shatters the complacency of those who languish in rockers and hurls them into unknown places;

We believe in the God of the Fourth Age, who carries with love those who can no longer walk where they wish, who listens with compassion to life stories of those who struggle to make sense of life at eventime; who hovers over the bedside of the frail, the weak, the dying, with whispers of a better country yet to be;

We believe in the God of all ages, who is ageless, and who dwells with people of every age.

*HYMN: "O Jesus, I Have Promised"

*BLESSING AND BENEDICTION

*Standing if able

Appendix D

Resolution on the International Year of Older Persons
Adopted by the General Assembly, Presbyterian Church (U.S.A.) 1998

C. Resolution on the International Year of Older Persons

Precis

25.0339

This resolution commends the United Nations for declaring 1999 as the International Year of Older Persons and offers the church encouragement to pursue appropriate ways for its recognition and celebration. It recognizes that the locus of ministry to older persons is at the congregational and middle governing body level and that the General Assembly is able to provide resources and raise the awareness of the church and society to the needs of older adults. The United States government is requested to address the needs and concerns of the nation's aging population as a priority. There is a request for a study and recommendations on what the ministry of caregiving will mean for church and society as the population rapidly ages and for those with debilitating and/or fatal illnesses.

1. Resolution

25.0340

Whereas, the 50th General Assembly of the United Nations has proclaimed 1999 the "International Year of Older Persons" with the theme of "Toward a Society for All Ages'"; and

25.0341

Whereas, the numbers of people in the world over sixty years old will triple over the next few decades and in the course of a few generations, the proportion of older persons aged sixty and above will increase from approximately 1 in 14 to 1 in 4; and

25.0342

Whereas, the aging of the global population represents one of the major achievements and at the same time poses one of the major challenges for the twenty-first century; and

25.0343

Whereas, life is a gift of God and aging is a natural part of living involving the whole life span from birth to death; and

25.0344

Whereas, the Presbyterian Church (U.S.A.) has expressed concern for the world's aging population and for older adults in adopting the "Report of the Task Force—Older Adult Ministry: Growing in the Abundant Life" (204th General Assembly (1992)); and

25.0345

Whereas, half of the members of the Presbyterian Church (U.S.A.) are over fifty years of age; and

25.0346

Whereas, there is great value and

need for the generations engaging in life sharing across generation lines; and
25.0347

Whereas, there are many retired ministers, Christian educators, and lay leaders who have spent most of their lives serving the church, and who have time, talents, and commitment with an eagerness to continue to serve; therefore, be it
25.0348

Resolved, That the Advisory Committee on Social Witness Policy (ACSWP) recommends that the 210th General Assembly (1998) of the Presbyterian Church (U.S.A.) do the following:
25.0349

a. Commend the United Nations for declaring 1999 the "International Year of Older Persons."
25.0350

b. Encourage the church to recognize and celebrate the United Nations' "International Year of Older Persons."
23.0351

c. Commend the work of the Office of Older Adult Ministry in the Presbyterian Church (U.S.A.) and its work in bringing attention to the gifts and needs of older adults and developing ministries with, by, and for older adults.
23.0352

d. Encourage Presbyterians who are involved in ministries with and for older persons to become members of the Presbyterian Older Adult Ministry Network, a covenant group in the Congregational Ministries Division.
25.0353

e. Encourage retired members of the church, including retired church professionals and lay leaders, to explore new opportunities for service in the church.
25.0354

f. Encourage congregations to engage in programs that bring the generations together for interaction and appreciation of persons of other generations.
25.0355

g. Encourage presbyteries and synods to support older adult ministry in congregations, provide opportunities for older adult ministry leadership development, and to provide resources.
25.0356

h. Encourage the theological seminaries to include courses in older adult ministry in their curriculum and to provide opportunities for exposure to older adult ministries through field education experience and internships.
25.0357

i. Request that the General Assembly Council designate the appropriate bodies of the church to make available appropriate materials to celebrate the "International Year of Older Persons," including materials on the United Nations' work and research on aging populations, such as the United Nations' Principles for Older Persons and International Plan of Action.
25.0358

j. Call upon the Advisory Committee on Social Witness Policy, in consultation with the General Assembly Council's Office on Older Adult Ministry, to study and develop a Resolution on the Ministry of Caregiving. This resolution is to explore what the ministry of caregiving means as the population rapidly ages, and especially, for those with de-bilitating and/or fatal illnesses. The findings and recommendations of the study will be reported no later than the 213th General Assembly (2001).

[Financial Implications: $6,545 (1999), $11,438 (2000), Per Capita Budget (GAC)]
25.0359
k. Direct the Stated Clerk to request that United States government agencies support the United Nations' efforts and cooperate with the "International Year of Older Persons" by making it a priority to address the needs and concerns of the nation's aging population and by working to develop a society for all ages.
25.0360
l. Direct the Stated Clerk to communicate this message to the United Nations general secretary, the president and secretary of state of the United States, and the United States ambassador to the United Nations.

2. Background

a. The Church

25.0361
Presbyterians began to look closely at the needs of our aging population in the 1970s. The 185th General Assembly (1973) of the UPCUSA adopted a report called "The Rights and Responsibilities of Older Persons." The 119th General Assembly (1979) of the PCUS adopted "Ministry with Aging." The 193rd General Assembly (1981) of the UPCUSA adopted "Abundant Life for Aging People." The 204th General Assembly (1992) adopted

the report, "Older Adult Ministry: Growing in the Abundant Life," which established the following seven priority issues for ministering to and with older adults:
(1) Education and Leader Development,
(2) Special Focus on [Older Adult Issues Among] Racial Ethnic Persons,
(3) Attention to Health Care and Housing,
(4) Education and Action Concerning Abuse of Older Adults,
(5) Emphasis on Intergenerational Experiences,
(6) Attention to Spirituality and Aging, and
(7) Global and Ecumenical Concerns. (Minutes, 1992, Part I, pp 1014–15)
25.0362
The Presbyterian Office on Aging was established at the Presbyterian Center in Atlanta in 1981, and continues to serve the church in its present form as the Office on Older Adult Ministries. In 1982 the Presbyterian Older Adult Network was founded and today it has about 250 members.
25.0363
More than one-half of the members of the Presbyterian Church (U.S.A.) are over fifty years of age. This percentage will increase as the church moves into the twenty-first century. The needs and demands of older adults in congregations will increase as the population of older adults increases. A challenge is present within the church to lay plans now to meet these growing needs. Fortunately, congregations and middle governing bodies are already involved in many ways reaching out to older persons both within their memberships and in their communities.

25.0364

Congregations are involved in older adult ministries providing opportunities for spiritual formation and development, social activities, home services, transportation, involvement in health care concerns, care for the caregivers, and taking the church to the homebound, among other ministries. Presbyteries and synods are also involved by providing educational events, training congregational leaders in older adult ministry, developing support networks, and through the provision of resources.

25.0365

The General Assembly provides resources for use across the church and seeks to raise awareness of the needs and the skills of older adults. The office provides nurture and support for the Presbyterian Older Adult Ministry Network, provides training events, shares information and ideas, and assists in initiating older adult ministry.

25.0366

Congregations and church staff at all levels are being challenged to meet the needs of older adults and affirm the process of maturing while maintaining ministries to young adults and children.

b. *The United Nations*

25.0367

The United Nations has long been concerned with the needs of the aging. In 1982 the United Nations General Assembly (UNGA) convened the "World Assembly on Aging" and in the same year endorsed the International Plan of Action on Aging. In 1990 the UN designated October 1 as the "International Day for the Elderly." In 1991 the United Nations General Assembly adopted the "Principles for Older Persons" and in 1992 the assembly adopted a strategy for the decade 1992–2001 called "Global Targets on Aging for the Year 2001."

25.0368

At its 50th General Assembly in 1995, the United Nations General Assembly decided to observe 1999 as the "International Year of Older Persons," "in recognition of humanity's demographic coming of age" and the promise that holds for "maturing attitudes and capabilities in social economic, cultural and spiritual undertakings" (UNGA Resolution 47/5). The theme of "Toward a Society for All Ages" reflects a growing concern for ensuring age integration. "Aging is a natural part of living, involving the whole lifespan from birth to death" (*Older Adult Ministry: Growing in the Abundant Life*, pp. 5–6). It "encompasses the situation of older persons, the individual's lifelong development, relationships between the generations, and the relationship between aging and the development of society" (UNGA Resolution 50/1114). A society for all ages seeks to empower the generations to contribute to one another and share in the fruits of their interaction, so that the potential and rights of all are realized.

25.0369

The objective of the year with older persons is to ensure that priority attention will be given to the situation of older persons and to promote the Principles for Older

Persons adopted by the UN General Assembly in 1991 (UNGA Resolution 46/91). The Principles are grouped around the themes of independence, participation, care, self-fulfillment, and dignity. Additionally, "preparation of the entire population for the later stages of life should be an integral part of social policies and encompass physical, psychological, cultural, religious, spiritual, economic, health and other factors." The promotion of these principles and additional factors will enhance the quality of life for all.

c. Challenges to Societies

25.0370

The World Bank reports that over the next few decades, the numbers of people in the world over sixty years old will triple, causing the global percentage of elderly to jump from 9 percent in 1990 to 16 percent in 2030. The result will be a global society that is by far the oldest in the history of the world. With rising incomes and medical advances, families have fewer children and people live longer, causing populations to age. As many in the aging population retire, they will experience the limited access to income that comes with retirement, increased health concerns, and health-care costs. While longevity is one of the greatest achievements of the twentieth century, the increase in the world's population will place unprecedented demands on societies to meet the needs of both old and young, rich and poor.

25.0371

Families have traditionally cared for their older family members. This is one method that societies have used to provide older persons with the support they may need during their later years. However, changes in economic, political and demographic environments have made family elder care less dependable than it has been in the past. Decreasing fertility rates result in fewer children to share the responsibility for caring for parents. Increased migration rates also make it less likely that children will live near their parents. The loss of family support networks can threaten the quality of these years for the individual, as well as burden unprepared societies beyond their capacities.

25.0372

When families can no longer provide care for older adults, governments may establish formal arrangements to provide for their support. It needs to be recognized that such support programs will require social investments. There are needs that cannot be met by government. The church and other voluntary organizations have responsibilities and opportunities in this situation.

25.0373

In the United States, life expectancy has increased by approximately twenty-eight years since 1900. In 1890, Americans over sixty-five years of age represented only 4 percent of the nation's population. By the late 1980s, the percentage had risen to about 12 percent. It is estimated that by 2050, as many as one in four Americans will be over sixty-five years of age. Government institutions, churches, nonprofit organizations, and families must begin to prepare appropriately to meet the challenges and possibilities present-

ed by our nation's aging population.
25.0374

Issues such as the dignity and quality of life and preserving life at any cost will need to be prayerfully considered. Concerned citizens will need to advocate for policies and institutions that ensure the well-being of all age groups. Our health care and social security systems will have to be adjusted to meet the demands of an aging society. Chronic diseases, such as cancer, heart, and lung diseases, are more likely to strike older persons and will occupy a large percentage of health care costs. Health-care systems will therefore have to address the rising costs of long-term care. The United States' Social Security system will be challenged by these changing conditions.
25.0375

Since women tend to live longer than men, they will comprise two-thirds of the aging population. They face greater issues of poverty as they age due to their gender status. Due to caretaking responsibilities and workplace discrimination, many women spend less time in the workforce, earn lower salaries, and therefore, have more limited access to pensions than do men. Elderly women are more likely to end up living alone. Many women marry men older than themselves and are less likely than men to remarry after loss of a spouse. There is likely to be a greater number of older women in need of care and concern as a result.
25.0376

Additionally, in many regions of the world, women lack economic security because they have no property rights and have limited access to inheritance. When a husband dies in Uganda, for instance, his relatives claim the household property, often evicting the widow and her children from the home.
25.0377

While the United States struggles to adapt current support systems and to address quality of life issues for its aging, the most pressing problem for the aging in developing countries will be to avoid poverty and even starvation. Because of the broad diffusion of medical knowledge and declining fertility, developing countries are aging far more rapidly and, thus, will be much poorer than industrialized countries are as their populations age. In addition, in many areas of the developing world, traditional family support systems have been drastically undermined due to urbanization, epidemics, wars, and famine.
25.0378

The church does not have to face this changing situation with despair. Challenging times call for people willing to seek new opportunities for ministry and creative possibilities for societal transformation. The increase in the world's population of older persons presents both the church and society with a critical opportunity to explore what life together in a new situation means.
25.0379

To fully realize the potential benefits inherent in the new moment, it is crucial for the church to explore and address certain issues that may be viewed as guideposts to discovering a new and different way of viewing life and death and especially the aging process. The Report of the Task Force on Older Adult Ministry, adopted by the 204th General Assembly (1992), *Older Adult Ministry: Growing in the Abundant Life*, frames a number of issues that, by shifting the focus of church members, may offer a better quality of life for all people. That report places an emphasis on community, interdependence, and intergenerational interchange rather than individuality, independence, and isolation from other age groups. It stresses reflection on the meaning of life, its relationships, and maturity and death as a part of one's life journey rather than living life on the surface without depth or meaning and on death as something to be denied and dreaded (*Older Adult Ministry: Growing in the Abundant Life*, Report of the Task Force on Older Adult Ministry, adopted by the 204th General Assembly (1992), p. 11).

25.0380

The Presbyterian Church (U.S.A.) is called to participate in an active way in the United Nations' "International Year for Older Persons." What better contribution can Presbyterians make to the support of the "International Year of Older Persons" than in developing new ways that bring people together! In many practical ways, Presbyterians and others can model the values that grow out of our biblical and theological faith tradition:

—to lead the way in developing a growing respect for the dignity of all persons, no matter what their age;

—to lead the way in helping persons to live the entire span of life abundantly, to the fullest extent of their capabilities;

—to shape values and attitudes in society, and to address issues concerning the meaning of life and the meaning of death;

—in its capability of utilizing the vast treasure of skills, wisdom, commitment, time, and energy to be found among its older adults in leading the church into the next century. (*Older Adult Ministry: Growing in the Abundant Life*. Report of the Task Force on Older Adult Ministry, adopted by the 204th General Assembly (1992), pp. 11–12)

Appendix E
National Organizations

Alzheimers Disease and Related Disorders Association, Inc.
919 N. Michigan Ave., Suite 1000
Chicago, IL 60611-1676

American Association of Homes and Services
   for the Aging
901 E St., NW, Suite 500
Washington, DC 20004-2837

American Association of Retired Persons (AARP)
601 E St., NW
Washington, DC 20049

American Society on Aging
833 Market St., Suite 511
San Francisco, CA 94103

Elderhostel
75 Federal St.
Boston, MA 02110

Gray Panthers
2025 Pennsylvania Ave., NW
Suite 821
Washington, DC 20006

National Association of Area Agencies on Aging
1112-16th St., NW, Suite 100
Washington, DC 20036

National Black Aging Network
1212 Broadway, Suite 830
Oakland, CA 94612

National Council on the Aging, Inc.
409 3rd St., SW
Washington, DC 20024

National Hospice Organization
1901 North Moore St., Suite 901
Arlington, VA 22209

National Interfaith Coalition on Aging
409 3rd St., SW
Washington, DC 20024

North American Association of Jewish Homes and Housing
   for the Aging
10830 North Central Expressway, Suite 150
Dallas, TX 75231-1022

Presbyterian Association of Homes for the Aging
510 N. Brookside Dr.
Little Rock, AR 72205-1694

Presbyterian Church (U.S.A.) Office of Older Adult Ministry
100 Witherspoon St.
Louisville, KY 40202-1396

Social Security Administration
6401 Security Blvd.
Baltimore, MD 21235

U.S. Congress Senate Special Committee on Aging
G-31 Dirksen Building
Washington, DC 20510-6400

"Aging News Alert," "Housing the Elderly Report,"
"Selling to Seniors," "Senior Law Report"
C.D. Publications
8204 Fenton St.
Silver Spring, MD 20910